God's Ruling Ballot

God's Ruling Ballot

Ideologies Beyond Legislative Enactments
United States of America
2016 Presidential Election Period

Rachel J. Wallace

ISBN: 978-0-578-75192-4

Table of Contents

Disclosure Statement

While the author made every effort to ensure the information in this book is correct, the author does not assume liability to any party for the outcomes, damages, or interventions caused by (1) misinterpretations of the text, (2) omissions within the text, and/or (3) coincidences between the text and associated information. Furthermore, the observations, perspectives, preferences, political views, action requests, and recommendations in this book are not intended to substitute laws, principles, or political or public obligations. In addition, the views herein are not those of any specific group, faith, culture, political party, fellowship, or organization. Consequently, the assessments, observations, and opinions regarding the Federal Bureau of Investigation (FBI), the White House, and other entities are solely my opinions and not of the FBI, the White House, or any associated entities. Lastly, the reader must determine how to act on the contents of this book without taking any risks beyond the law, the reader's competence, or the reader's comfort level.

Preface

Being a college graduate with a business management and communication degree, a former analyst for the Federal Bureau of Investigation, and an open-minded, concerned, and patriotic citizen of the United States, I must renounce the tactics, obstructions, and disorders that I observed in the 2016 election period.

The United States never had a presidential election period like that of 2016.

If the American flag had wings, it would have flown away; if the Statue of Liberty could exhale, she would blow out her flaming torch; and if God himself had to come back to vote, he would have rebuked the entire election.

Nevertheless, fear not. The American flag still blows proud and freely, the Statue of Liberty still holds her flaming torch, and God remains merciful.

Still, this election galvanized a division within the US homeland, populations, allies, associates, and establishments.

Moreover, what was to transpire later was so outrageous that it compelled me to write this book to incite a call to restore order to our country and mend our democracy.

In the meantime, I will not point a finger at the people to blame for this division but must hold them liable for the indignities that emerged throughout this election period.

Everyone realizes how they motivated, allowed, and strengthened these ignominies. I hope my perceptiveness gives them the incentive to redeem themselves.

Let us start with how shameful it was to watch members of the US Congress deny the offensive attacks on US intelligence agencies and disregard the highly respected officials who devoted the best segments of their lives to protecting the nation and the structure of our republic.

Irrefutably, certain representatives of the US Congress, fearful of their own re-election prospects, fell silent when it was vital to defend intelligence agencies, the rule of law, and decent generals. Their self-imposed boundaries resulted in a Congress that ensued as a contaminated assembly.

To further contaminate the political atmosphere, a 2016 presidential candidate, during their rallies, inspired the crowd to shout disparaging chants about their challengers. This tactic gave the candidate a way to validate their devotees' loyalty.

The problem is, again, Congress turned a blind eye to this conduct.[1]

Congress needs to evaluate the lack of concern exhibited during this election period to bring about a reputable and cooperative union as an alternative to making congresspersons more hostile toward each other and less likely to compromise and work together; the relationships were damaged.

Congress should establish a statutory order of protection for US intelligence agencies to prevent them from being desecrated by their own leadership—like when the reputations of intelligence agencies were attacked for reporting that the US election was encumbered by a foreign rival, Russia.

If the President of the United States (POTUS), the US government, and other elected officials within the country would enact a percentage of what is conveyed in this book, they would be astonished how much it would improve the probability of our country succeeding as a distinguished nation once again!

Nevertheless, the sequence of events documented in this book articulates an array of complications that pushed the United States to become a country of turmoil and disgrace.

We have a duty to recommence and recover the con-

---

1 The conventions, code of behaviors, advice, and solutions in this book are targeted for a president, but they are similarly suitable for presidential candidates, vice presidents, future appointed and nominated officials, and executive office bearers.

gregation of this wonderful country to prevent it from sinking into the foundation on which it was built to stand.

Therefore, if you want to help avoid the collapse of this amazing country, you must not ignore this obligation, or there might be plenty of tears shed to sink the entire nation.

Wall of Reason
What is the rationale for building a wall for protection
if the greatest risks are instigated by the builder on their side of
the wall?
–RJW

Let us be clear: crimes and obstructions occur in many cities and communities, at home and abroad, by people of every diverse and ethnical background. When a crime is performed by an individual or group, they must be held liable for their crime. However, not everybody of that ethnicity should be held in contempt for the crime. Therefore, building a wall will never stop and hinder criminals, nor will it keep every offender in the world on the other side of a city, country, or community. Furthermore, who wants to feel like they are caged in or living under the control of a regime? A good leader would not revile anyone for aspiring to live a fully embraced life as opposed to an unsafe or sheltered one.

The United States is a free country, and its inhabitants refuse to be enslaved by division or disheartening prejudices within the borders of any walls!

With that being said, I ask that you set aside your pride and magnify your heart to explore my philosophies and expectations to restore the magnificence of this country.

Rachel J. Wallace (RJW)

1
Promising Allegiances

**There is no exception to the rule documented
for breaching an oath you have vowed to obey.**

–RJW

I am not an advocate or representative for any specific group, institution, or union. I am essentially a private citizen who holds a high regard for my country and has robust faith in freedom, liberty, and justice for all. Nonetheless, I worked as a civilian employee for thirty years (now retired) for the Federal Bureau of Investigation (FBI). This well-regarded agency enhanced my competencies and specialized skills by teaching me the worth of integrity, consideration, and dependability.

When I entered the FBI, I took an oath to protect and serve my country and to exemplify the fidelity, bravery, and integrity of the organization. It was made clear that if I breached any aspect of my pledge, I would be dismissed and possibly prosecuted. I upheld the oath from the day I raised my hand to take that pledge until the day I raised the same hand to take my exit oath, when I retired.

Still, the oaths taken by presidents, members of Congress, and other high-level officials are more complex than those taken by federal administrative and logistic personnel. Regardless of the judicial, legislative, and executive branches of the government at the (federal, state, or local) levels to which an individual applies, an inquiry into his or her possessions, criminal background, and acquaintances must be made to validate the individual's suitability to work in public service.

If the investigation concludes that an individual is in acceptable standing, that individual is appropriate to be hired. Once hired, individuals must take an oath to fulfill their obligations.

However, before any employees can acquire or keep a security clearance, they are required to complete the Questionnaire for National Security Positions on an annual basis and adhere to ethics obligations.

The FBI is precise about its employees receiving and maintaining appropriate security clearances. In fact, if employees omit information required to be disclosed in their questionnaire or provide deceitful information concerning ethics, they can be fired and/or indicted for lying.

Although as an FBI employee I had adequate security clearances, every so often I had to obtain additional security clearances to gain access to high-profile projects. Even then, access was contingent on a need-to-know basis.

While I have worked in several FBI units and divisions, I spent most of my career in the Counterintelligence and Intelligence Services Division. Although the responsibilities for each of my assignments were interesting and significant, the following were the most memorable of my endeavors:

- compiling and arranging data for the directors' daily reports and presidential briefings
- being deployed to Baton Rouge, Louisiana, in 2004 to provide logistical support for the FBI's central command post in the aftermath of Hurricane Katrina
- working on the operational task forces for the 9/11 attacks and for the DC sniper investigation
- acquiring training for more than three hundred FBI senior managers and organizational and contractual personnel

However, the highlights of my career were:

- receiving a telephone call from President Obama's National Security Staff regarding a job interview
- taking a picture with the Honorable John Walsh of *America's Most Wanted*
- receiving a reward from the FBI's Employee Suggestion Program for my recommendations on

how and why to modify security protocols for the FBI's workforce after the 1995 Oklahoma City bombing, and

- receiving an award from the FBI's American Legion Post 56 association for the advancement of their membership.

I'd be remiss not to mention how elating it was to shake hands with the forty-third POTUS, George W. Bush, when he came to FBI headquarters to acknowledge the employees of the organization for their work in support of the 9/11 investigation.

2
Steadfast Values and Protocols

Ask God for the strength to endure your obligations if you shall weaken amid your tasks.

–RJW

I am known to be meticulous regarding the progression and enhancement of policy and procedure, but my skills in policy and procedure development are outside the sphere of political policy making. Still, I do not need to be a rocket scientist to know when a democratic organization needs a definitive conversion.

Congress is obligated to protect certain aspects of the US democracy in the manner it was formed to function.

However, throughout the 2016 period, there were

enormous inappropriate protests, obstructions, and portrayals that subdued the very essence of what Congress was intended to safeguard. Therefore, US policy makers need to stress how crucial it is for legitimacy to be exemplified by every person who participates in a presidential race or other US election.

In addition, it should be mandatory for every participant in a political election to be meticulously cognizant of the details of the Constitution, military paradigms and protocols, and the fundamental laws that ensure liberty and justice for all.

Otherwise, someone oblivious to the Constitution, uninformed about the military, and intolerant of diversity could be the next POTUS.

Also, candidates should be required to submit a five-thousand-word dissertation that answers the following:

- What is the full obligation of the US Constitution?
- How is the Constitution a shield of protection for a person's civil rights? How would you preserve these rights and the fairness of these rights?
- What would you change about the Constitution? And why?
- Describe the three immediate methods of action you would consider in a global catastrophe?
- What is the focal entity that you would rely upon as a primary basis in a detrimental situation regarding the country?

Then authorized assessors would classify the responses as "honorable," "dishonorable," or "objectionable." At this point, authorized assessors would rank the responses to begin the omission process. Subsequently, the lowest-ranked aspirants would be asked to vacate their candidacy, of course, with supportable explanation.

3
Armor of Protection

**God is the master and ruler of the world;
man will never equate to his authority.**

–RJW

The ideologies presented in this book are solely my philosophies, and they are by no means projected to disrespect the divine or political views or theories of others.

*Contrary to perspectives, it requires a God-given person
to lead a country.*

–RJW

The divine verses below are portrayed to reinforce my

overall message. They are cited from the New Testament: Exodus, Ten Commandments; Ephesians; and John (King James).

"I am the Lord your God" (Exodus 20, Ten Commandments).

"You shall have no other Gods before me" (Exodus 20, Ten Commandments).

"You shall not give false testimony against your neighbor" (Exodus 20, Ten Commandments).

That He would grant you, according to the riches of His glory, to be strengthened with might through His Spirit in the inner man, that Christ may dwell in your hearts through faith; that you, being rooted and grounded in love, may be able to comprehend with the saints. (Ephesians 3:16–18)

"These things I have spoken to you, that in Me you may have peace. In the world you will have tribulation: but be of good cheer; I have overcome the world" (John 16:33).

God's tranquility is our passageway through the world.
–RJW

God molded us distinctly but equally. So, it is unrealistic for anyone to think they are of more treasure than their neighbor.

Besides, the commencement of God's creations was foreseen to be fulfilling for the whole world.

*We must unravel the kinks in our knots before we unravel the
weaves of another's.*
–RJW

Regardless of who you are or what the limitations of your
vicinities may be, if an explosion were to happen in a crowd
of people (God forbid), everybody in the crowd would be
traumatized, hurt, or killed.

*We are bounded in the array of God's orb;
therefore, whatsoever happens in the world impacts us all.*
–RJW

A few folks can nonchalantly deal with complications,
whereas others have a tougher time coping with a hard-
ship.

*God gives us the willpower to defeat difficulties. Therefore,
surrendering to life's difficulties deters us from our purpose and
isolates us from the rest of the world.*
–RJW

In our lifetime, it is unlikely we will meet everybody in
the world or even twice meet the same individual. So it is
virtuous to be the genuine and good-natured person that
you are created to be. It gratifies God to see his formations
of magnificence.

Kindness is a workout for the heart to keep it beating with compassion.

–RJW

When you meet someone who seems low-spirited, say, "Hello." Ask, "How are you?" Or offer, "Have a blessed day."[2]

That person might be grieving, be having zilch to smile about, or just be experiencing a bad day, and a flash of kindness might interpose their worst of thoughts.

Yet don't be dissuaded if that person is not responsive to your civility. Extend that courtesy to someone else. Eventually, you will get pleasant results.

If you show kindness far and wide, it comes back full circle.

–RJW

Whenever you attempt to encourage others, it displays thankfulness for the solaces God has provided to you.

It would be reprehensible for favor to become inexistent.

–RJW

---

2   Explore with vigilance, rationality, and parental guidance for those under eighteen years old.

4
Wearing the Crown

**Beauty goes beyond makeup, fashion, fortune, or fame;
it is the bare bones of a person's character that individualizes
their beauty.**
–RJW

Beauty pageants, talent shows, and other real-world challenges include judging panels. Usually, these judges are required to assess the uniqueness, aptitude, and vision of the contestants.

From the 1970s through the 1990s, I competed in several fashion shows, talent shows, and two pageants, Miss Congeniality and Miss Photogenic. Even though I did not win first place in these challenges, my photographs are illustrated in two distinctive magazine publications.

Nonetheless, at the end of each of these competitions, I felt like a winner because I learned how to endure and respect a multiplicity of opinions and values from a diversified assembly.

This brought me to the conclusion that a contest is a rational assessment of diverse partakers whose aspiration is to achieve an objective that validates their worthiness to be crowned for a certain representation.

Bearing in mind my rationalization of a contest, a political competition can be equated with a beauty pageant, fashion show, talent show, and similar competitions since they all involve the incentive of "wearing the crown".

An antagonistic demeanor is toxic to an appealing ether,
as arrogance is draining to a rejoiced ambience.
–RJW

5
Constitutional Reliance

**It takes one to initiate an act of faith.
The faith of many will instigate and uphold the bond of a
nation.
–RJW**

A president must obey the laws of the land in all situations. Moreover, a president should not alter the law in retaliation, in distress, or to execute personal vendettas.

*Anyone who pursues power for personal benefit
fails to exemplify the essence of a moral leader.*
–RJW

A president should explain how their decisions are accommodating to the mainstream of the country, and the president must evaluate the feedback they receive from those decisions.

If enormous partings, misperceptions, protests, and violence are the outcomes, the president ought to reconsider those decisions to prevent further mayhem.

Reasonableness produces succeeding respect; empathy gives solace.
–RJW

Furthermore, presidents ought to be yielding to the criticisms articulated by their staffers; federal, state, and local representatives; and other upstanding citizens.

It is okay to modify your perceptions with one proviso: the changes are not masked by alternative facts.
–RJW

When manifestations of hate crimes, terrorizations, and violence emerge, a commander in chief is expected to condemn these materializations and their offenders with a steadfast and firm perseverance.

Honorable leaders will thwart a vulgar battle without pursuing violence for those they have sworn to defend.
–RJW

Take a pause, and ask yourself, "Does the president

have the capability and valor to preserve and lead the country in a worldwide catastrophe?" If it is challenging to answer the above question, either you are not confident about your president's dependability or just disregarded it. Nevertheless, you can contemplate how you would rather answer this question prior to casting your vote for the next election.

When you elect political candidates, you are agreeing to their choices too!

–RJW

6
Distinctively Chosen

Being capable of achieving a duty is rewarding;
being incapable of achieving a task is inadequate!
–RJW

The FBI affords additional training for employees to make sure they are current with state-of-the-art data and technology.

I can attest to the above statement since the core of my profession with the FBI involved training. Still, I always aspired to exceed above and beyond what was expected to accomplish my tasks. But this did not make me eligible to become the US Secretary of State or the POTUS!

Why hire a retired bus driver to fly a plane
when it is more practical to hire a former pilot?
–RJW

If someone is selected for a distinctive job, that person must be capable of doing the work. Though, it is possible for anyone to become proficient in a profession with the proper edification.

Case in point, it is more logical to board a bus driven by a former pilot than to board an airplane flown by a current chauffeur. While I support equal employment opportunities and the Fair Labor Standards Act, everybody is not fit to pilot a plane, drive a bus, instruct a student, or become the POTUS!

Teachers are predestined to teach, preachers are ordained to
preach, and presidents and Congresspersons are duty bound to
uphold the declarations of the Constitution.
–RJW

Perhaps educational establishments will expand their tactics to increase a scholar's knowledge of the ignominies that emerged in the 2016 election era.

A progressive comprehension of the indignities that occurred in this period will help forthcoming representatives circumvent these same complications. (Expectantly, this book will contribute to that effort.)

Besides, anyone who partakes in the political establishment ought to be aware of the objectivities entailed in the wide-ranging orders of politics.

I asked my four-year-old niece, "What are you going to be when you grow up?" and "Who are you going to be for Halloween?" She said, "I'm going to be an FBI agent. My name is going to be Princess Agent 99." Then she said, "I'm going to be Wonder Woman for Halloween!"

Her responses projected that she assumes to be an influential, dedicated, loyal patron to society.

I asked my eight-year-old nephew the same questions. He replied, "I'm going to be a pop star for Halloween and a doctor when I'm grown up."

Fifteen years later, he was working at a hospital sanitizing and prepping rooms for incoming patients. Later, he received a promotion. He began working with surgeons, sterilizing the medical instruments before and after surgeries.

Although he did not become a doctor, he was still in the arena of saving lives! This shows that he was steadfast to his youthful aspirations.

When a child emulates distinguished beings or characters, they are enthused by an image, character, or behavior. That is why it is vital to observe the individualities a child is contented with and attentive to.

You should not coach a child to be an athlete if the child yearns to sing. It will be advantageous to register that child for vocal lessons, school chorus, or church choir.

It is prudent to be mindful of the influential characters

children are susceptible to, especially if those characters are not of respectable quality or it can diminish a child's perspective of whom to embody.

7
Presidential Heroes

**Humans are not flawless,
but a leader's flaws must not blemish their leadership.**

–RJW

Presidents Bill Clinton (1993–2001) and Barack Obama (2008–2016) are my presidential heroes! Encouragingly, they have demonstrated a perceptiveness of what characterizes a reasonable commander in chief.

In my heart of hearts, it would have been extremely reassuring if either of these men were leading the country at the time the 9/11 attacks occurred. When 9/11 befell, I was at work at FBI headquarters in Washington, DC. When we evacuated, I remember roaming the streets, lost in the masses, feeling as though the world was ending. Every federal, state, local, and private establishment was evacuated, and the streets were extremely congested.

Once the crowds dissipated, it became a ghost town. I sauntered through the streets feeling isolated and confused, hoping that my commuter bus might show up.

After an hour or so, there were no buses in sight. I walked four blocks to Fourteenth and G Street NW to see if maybe the bus had taken an alternate route. Unfortunately, there was no inkling that buses were traveling about at all.

As I walked away from the bus stop in a daze, a gentleman approached me and asked, "Ma'am, are you okay?"

I responded, "No. I was supposed to meet my sister two hours ago, but I think all entrances into DC are blocked. I can't call her because the phones are inoperable."

The gentleman said, "I'm a manager at a restaurant. I had to evacuate my employees as a safety precaution, so I cannot invite you in, but people are still across the street at the cigar bar. Let us go over there. I'll ask my buddy if you can use his landline to call your sister."

When we entered the cigar bar, the gentleman walked up to his friend the bar owner and asked if his phone was working.

He said, "No. Sorry, the phones are still down." Then this generous man asked me if I would like to have something to eat.

I responded, "No, thank you."

He said, "How about you get something from the café

on the corner? They are still open. Plus, you need to sit down, relax, and rest your feet. They look swollen."

I said, "Thank you, but that's okay."

He retorted, "You don't know how long you'll be stuck here before you get a ride home. Tell you what, take these twenty dollars, and get yourself something to eat before the café closes. God bless you, and please be safe."

It is astounding how this stranger's thoughtfulness distracted me from the emotional and distressing state of mind I was in several hours earlier.

A couple of weeks later, I went to this gentleman's restaurant to repay him. When I walked in, he was standing near the bar. I walked up, excused myself, and handed him a twenty-dollar bill.

He said, "Hi! Good to see you. I wasn't expecting this back."

I replied, "I know, but thanks again for everything."

Back to president number forty-four, Mr. Barack Obama. Not only was he the youngest POTUS, he was also the first African American POTUS.

Unfortunately, President Obama met multiple instances of discrimination as an African American president, mainly because his nationality was being challenged by several individuals who pursued attempts to discredit his earned victory. Yet, their unproven prevarications did not hinder President Obama from managing the nation in a virtuoso manner.

Without a doubt, I rightly believe that President Obama was destined to safeguard our nation and projected to do so through his candid endeavors preceding his presidency.

President Obama's principles, fervor, and sense of duty were undeniably suitable to preserving the country from anticipated mayhem and devastating rivals. For example, the assassination of Osama bin Laden was achieved during President Obama's term as the commander in chief. While this was not the crowning achievement of his presidency, it was a vital undertaking regarding the security of our country.

President Obama's sense of obligation to the United States established a suitable and celebrated legacy for the country for years to come.

I look onward to seeing statues and portraits of President Barack Obama and the First Lady Michelle Obama in institutions far and wide throughout the world.

8
Respectful Deliberations

**People should have approbation for themselves;
but when they do not have respect for a multiplicity of human beings,
they will have miniscule deference for a few.
–RJW**

Those who intentionally make hostile, deceitful declarations about someone to cause detriment to their character is blameworthy for initiating atrocious acts of defamation and provocation.

Therefore, this subsequent directive ought to be enacted for those who partake in a political or communal decision-making assembly: "Incivilities or deceptions regarding a competitor is *prohibited*. Identified aggressors will be excluded from all administrative or democratic involvement and perhaps penalized for their odious conduct."

Political debates are presumed to be (1) a platform that permits candidates to convey views about policies and issues relating to the country and its citizens and (2) a stage to openly voice views about other candidates' perspectives.

It is okay for contenders to voice their opinion about any chaotic, hindering, or illicit actions performed by challengers or elected officials currently in office, but it must be expressed candidly, not as an antagonistic attack.

Nevertheless, no assertion in the US Constitution or verse in the holy Bible encourages physical attacks or verbal attacks if somebody does not see eye to eye with someone else.

Even though the US Constitution sanctions freedom of speech, there are no guarantees that people will speak appropriately or honestly. However, we expect those who take an oath to defend civil liberties and protect human rights to always speak appropriately and truthfully.

Generally, we should be enthralled by catchphrases, ads, and endorsements exemplified by political candidates, politicians, and other elected officials. These campaign communication strategies are essential, since they convey the viewpoints, incentives, and characteristics of the hopefuls.

9
Speak Now

You must cease divergences in advance,
or you will entertain a world of agonies in the end.
–RJW

Observing the induction of an incoming president is comparable to witnessing vows at a wedding ceremony, except a president's vows are dedicated to the nation. Surely, the president is making a promise to the nation for better or worse, whether richer or poorer.

Traditionally, people are permitted to speak up to challenge a marriage. If no one wants to contest the matrimony, the marriage proceeds and becomes official. Nevertheless, if one of the marital partners breaches their given vows, the marriage can be annulled.

The "speak now" tradition is a good technique to use for the confirmation of magistrates, administrators, lawful officers, legislatures, representatives, and additional political partakers. Still, it is necessary to first prove allegations before discounting somebody for a confirmation. However, if officials are proven to be accountable of a wrongdoing, they must be detached from all public, executive, and lawful duties before any further exposure of their offense is discovered. Otherwise, the extra exposure will become a nuisance for the country, the citizens, and the democracy.

It is typical for us to make mistakes, but we must be accountable for our faults.

−RJW

10
Liberation of Equality

We need to have a certain acuity for someone's feasibility but also need someone to reverence ours.

–RJW

Parents envision the future they want for their children during adolescence. But then, once the children are grown, they are free to choose the lifestyle they desire. While we respect our parents' desires, sometimes their anticipations are not well matched with our aspirations. Nonetheless, we still deliberate and share our ambitions with them. But if we are uncertain about our ambitions, we can always ask God to navigate us toward our needs and trust him to supply them.

Having a vision is the vantage point of projecting the future.
–RJW

The Constitution is a guard against the chastisement of folks because of their values and individual preferences.

No one should make perpetual attempts to criminalize any aspect of an individual's lifestyle, including whom a person can love, whether a woman must bear a child, a person's privileges to use public restrooms, or a person's military participation. Therefore, the moral advancement of an individual should not be measured, limited, or precluded because of any aspect of that person's individuality.

Society needs to be respectful of the infinite differences of a
revolutionizing world.
–RJW

Historically, various cultures were not allowed to convey their views or stand up for their civic rights because of the restrictions and terrorization they would encounter.

Eventually, laws were established that give people the freedom to speak, within a realm of reasonable restrictions. Despite that, still to this day, those rights are repeatedly being denied by unreasonable antagonists who should be compliant with the impartiality of civilization by now.

It is characteristic of people to express their point of

view about matters that concern them, that they are privy to, or that they may differ with. Even so, it is imperative those views are nondiscriminatory to another's values, life, or livelihood.

Still, there have been endless deep-seated disrespects throughout the 2016 cataclysm, such as thoughtless efforts to debacle the Obama Affordable Care Act (Obamacare); the confounding separation and deportation of numerous people of various ethnicities and their families; unlawful and brazen shooting incidences and the resulting demises; segregation of cultures; the imprudent limitations imposed on the rights of the LGBTQ community; and heartless sexual coercions, abuses, and revelations.

Let us assess some of the complications of the aforesaid matters, starting with Obamacare.

Obamacare

The dynamic efforts to eliminate Obamacare during the 2016 election period were divisive for the country and citizens. Generally, it was a mayhem contrived at the expense of peoples' lives and deaths.

Certain folks could not care less about the grandiosities, ruses, and controversies involving politics, but most everybody is concerned about their well-being, medical care, and medical expenses.

The scarceness of one's healthiness is flattering to endangerment.
—RJW

What the current administration and Congress needed to do was (1) improve the existing health-care coverage for persons with chronic and perilous health conditions and (2) decrease or eliminate the cost for folks who couldn't manage to pay for health care or treatment at all. These changes would still be beneficial today.

It would also be comprehensible for the new administration and Congress to consider including former President Obama's contribution to any changes since his devotion to his country and desire to make things better for Americans, has always been resolute.

The Transgendered Community's Restricted Access

Congress must take part in eradicating the continuous restrictions regarding the rights of the LGBTQ community, and the transgendered community in particular, to use communal restrooms. While the other subsets of the LGBTQ community, as well as other members of society, are concerned with this issue, it affects the transgendered community the most directly.

A sensible resolution is for the POTUS, in consensus with US representatives and the communal establishments, to execute a directive that would make public bathrooms appropriate regardless of gender. The bathrooms can be designed like those at public gas stations, hospitals, public transportation, various stores, and restaurants. These restrooms are usually characterized as unisex.

Animals have some of the same rights and indulgences that humans have. For instance, they have laws that safeguard them from being mistreated, as well as a variety of fashionable attire to wear; wellness spas; pet sitters; parks and communal areas for enjoyment and bathroom usage. Also, animals have a kindred love for human beings, and humans have the same affection for animals and accept them as members of their family. However, if these animals recognized some of the restrictions and cruelties imposed upon human beings, it would sadden them.

LGBTQ Military Liberties

Anytime individuals put their lives in jeopardy to serve and protect people and the country, they are champions and deserve the utmost reverence for their valor, sacrifices, and dedication.

Furthermore, any individuals who have such a firm commitment to their country, regardless of their gender, must be protected by constitutional laws that prevent them from being disparaged or prohibited to serve God, man, and country. The deliberate disregard for them or inattentions of these provisions is outrageous to the affected individuals and to the nation.

If the US Congress does not remedy these military concerns swiftly, it may find itself attempting to force folks to join the military. This will compromise the freedom and evolution of America's principles and advantages. Certainly, there is no desire to regress back to this passé stage in American history!

An individual's sexual preference is inexorable. Consequently, we should accept a person's predisposition with impartiality and reciprocal reverence.

For example, when a same-sex couple wants to get married and seeks out a wedding cake service for that marriage, to avoid misunderstandings, an amiable consideration must be established in advance.

Basically, US representatives ought to enact laws that require communal businesses that provide a communal service to mates to stipulate the range of that service by using statements like "we accommodate same-sex couples" or "we serve all couples." This would eradicate confusion, divergences, and uncertainties. It would also shield the civil rights of business owners, patrons, and society.

Consequently, if a POTUS and Congress were to contemplate enacting some of the recommendations in this book, it would stabilize everyone's civil liberties.

Sexual Transgressions

Numerous sexual infringements were exposed during the 2016 election period. These exposures incriminated various politicians, well-known personalities, entities, and establishments.

Even though these various revelations were obvious, evident, and outrageous, they were overlooked or minimized.

Unfortunately, sexual cruelties occur all over the world. However, the Me Too movement gives victims a new voice and protection platform to help reveal their abuses and defend their rights. This platform ultimately gives victims a solidity to discuss their abuses and reveal their aggressors.

The message I want to convey about inappropriate sexual conduct is as follows: whenever people furtively engage in sensual activities and one or both are married, it is simply infidelity.

However, when someone negotiates money or shows favoritism to keep a relationship concealed, to get or keep an influential job, or to sustain a decent status in society, they are committing a conspiracy as well bribery.

11

Essentials of Veracity

Journalists are the onlookers of the world, fervent emissaries, practicality conveyers, and moderate executors of candor.

–RJW

Our parents and grandparents often talked about how they communicated with society in the 1900s, which was often more complex than the means that we have for communicating these days. Receiving messages nowadays has progressed a thousand times over since then.[3]

My parents specified how they would convey messages

---

3   Compliments to the communication services, technical experts, and postal deliverers for evolving with technology.

via word of mouth and person-to-person communication. Occasionally, when they received messages about a birth, marriage, or demise, it was either outdated or wrong.

> *There is a pervasiveness of "not shooting the messenger."*
> *–RJW*

Today's hi-tech methods keep society apprised of what is going on all over the world. Still, people have their preference on how they wish to receive and circulate information, although newscasters seem to be the most dependable source for obtaining the facts and current updates.

We depend on the morality of those who have professed to be trustworthy to the public and disavow those who deliberately make statements and proclaim it to be true. Besides, anyone who purposely misleads their listeners is imposing a disgraceful ruse on society.

> *Twisting the truth is comparable to, but worse than, telling a twisted lie!*
> *–RJW*

Nonetheless, authentic newscasters and networks will unfalteringly rectify improper specifics that are meted out to the public to uphold the populace's confidence and avoid depreciation of their journalistic integrity.

12
Societal Temptations and Vibrant Tribulations

Disingenuous postings go viral faster than accurate news and facts.

–RJW

Social media covers a massive range of accessible information that provokes exchanges amid a diverse society. It also has a reputation for spreading the news more readily than making a telephone call.

When you are unable to contact your family and friends in a detrimental situation, you might see a bulletin via social media that's either imprecise or deceiving. This would be an ideal time to rely on the trustworthy newscasters to obtain precise information.

Most of us have heard or even have witnessed uncountable stories of how people use social media to (1) circulate, exhibit, and create offensive posts as well as (2) to network and develop hostile associations.

While social media is an essential resource, the most typical and sociable means to personally interact is the good old telephone. Though, it is not the best resource for verifying facts, especially if the conversation is based on gossip or falsehoods, unless the conversation is documented or there are discussions about corruption, intimidation, or further lawbreaking matters. Then, the conversation could be used as evidence.

Imagine just how detrimental it would be if the POTUS talked on the phone or sent transcripts and texts without secured restrictions, then made efforts to cover it up.

Besides, it is wrong for a president to focus on social media as a primary means of interacting with the nation and society.

Presidents inherit a complex status quo. So, every time they relinquish their time to address the country or send messages, apart from disasters, we ought to feel honored—but only if the messages are reassuring, reverential, and reciprocal, such as

- Wishing you a Safe holiday,
- Congratulations to the United States on their big win,

- The United States is with you in this time of tragedy, and
- This is a state of emergency, so follow the alternative measures directed by your governor and local officials.

Whether it's a disaster or glorifying affair, a president ought to constantly convey communications with sincerity and reverence irrespective of which option they exploit.

Besides, the best time for a president to be a social media enthusiast or entertain a social fan base is at the end of their tenure as commander in chief. Folks are delighted to network with and get advice from past presidents, especially if they have flourished as reputable leaders.

13
Tread Lightly in Revered Places

To establish a legacy, you must be worthy.
–RJW

*C*lick...*click*...*click*...*click*...*click* is all that I heard as I walked through halls of the White House for the first time. I had to pause and savor this moment of serenity and bliss in this influential dwelling.

My venture at the White House was in 2013 after getting a phone call from a member of President Obama's National Security Staff (NSS) requesting my presence at the White House to interview for a two-year detail assignment in the NSS. The most momentous experience of my FBI career!

The day of my interview, I merged in with the rushed mass on Pennsylvania Avenue, which was normal, except the ambience was significantly new that morning. Then again, I was on my way to the White House!

As I walked, I pondered: "Am I going to be face to face with the POTUS? Will I get to meet Mrs. Obama too? I hope the NSS staff is as convivial in person as on the phone. God knows, I hope I am selected for the job. I can put up with this morning bliss for the next two years!"

When I got closer to the White House, there were two Secret Service Officers (SSOs) standing at the gate. I gave one of the SSOs my credentials and invitation to the White House NSS. Then, I was directed to the security checkpoint.

Once I was cleared to proceed through the security gate, I walked through a pathway on the grasslands of the White House. My heart raced as I cross the threshold of the premises.

Next, I found myself strolling down a lengthy corridor complimented by tall ceilings. I had to pause and regain my composure. It felt as though angels were observing me from every corner of those high ceilings. Unexpectedly, an epiphany overcame me, and I began to pray this prayer: "God, bless all the presidents who've justly reigned in this mystical palace, and even if I don't get the job, thank you for bestowing this blessing on me. Amen!"

I kept down the hall and noticed there was a restroom in the right corridor. I went inside and washed my hands. Then I glimpsed in the mirror and said to myself, "I'm at the White House for a job interview. I can't believe it!"

When I exited the restroom, I checked the instructions for my interview and realized I was in the wrong corridor. As I walked to the next corridor, I saw two men standing in the hallway. The clicking of my heels became inaudible; I was soundlessly walking on a cloud.

In a resonant tone, one of the men welcomed me, "You must be Ms. Wallace."

I answered, "Yes. I am!"

After the formal introductions, one of the men guided me to a quaint office furnished with white patterned chairs adjacent to a matching couch. I was led to take a seat on the couch.

The interview took forty-five minutes. At the end, I thanked the interviewers and told them how much of an honor it was to be at the White House and to meet them. As I was leaving, I thought, "That went very well!"

Ultimately, the White House is the nation's sanctuary and fortress. Everyone who has the opportunity or privilege to cross the threshold of this divine dwelling has an obligation to have clean hands and an uncontaminated heart. Also, you need to tread lightly on these sacred grounds to savor the essence that dwells within.

I am certain the essence of worthy US presidents will forever be extant in the White House to preserve every virtuous thing about it! Besides, a malicious spirit cannot be still in the White House or rest serenely under its roof for an extended period. The precious spirits will not allow it.

14
Bravery and Honor

**Allowing an intolerable person to lead a nation is
like letting bears oversee lion cubs.**

–RJW

I need to address some of the unacceptable attempts to tarnish the reputation of US officials and intelligence agencies during the 2016 administration.

Foremost, the FBI is the "lily" of dynamic, lawful dependency. The dynamisms of the FBI authenticate its distinguished abilities to stand on its own merits.

Furthermore, if a POTUS were to handpick someone external to be the new FBI director or to lead any federal or law enforcement agency, that person had better have a stupendous camaraderie with that agency.

It would be reprehensible to appoint somebody with no expertise of how to lead this distinguished organization.

Besides, if an existing director is not a threat to the country or the agency, that director should continue in the position to oversee and procure the progress of organizational proficiency.

When you try fixing something that is not broken,
it is a bigger mess trying to repair it.
–RJW

Also, it would be imprudent to compel a US federal agency to amalgamate with a political administration or its complexities—mainly because federal agencies and additional government agencies were designed to operate independently, for good reason.

Besides, mixing a federal agency's line of work with a political administration would certainly be nonconforming to the responsibilities and mission of each organization. If you examine the history of most of the federal, state, and local agencies and public and private organizations, you will learn conspiracies and betrayals have occurred in every one of them.

Clearly, it is public knowledge that the FBI has encountered some adversities throughout the years for perplexing reasons—mostly because the people do not honor the pledges they have avowed to obey. Whereas honest individuals keep their solemn word.

Nonetheless, I can justly avow, "When the FBI encounters imprudence and disloyalty, it is driven to rectify the matters in addition to persevering in its profession and mission."

My FBI Experience

After graduating from high school, I went to an industrial business college. While enrolled, I applied for some jobs at federal and state agencies.

Several months later, I got notification that I qualified for quite a few of the jobs but only took interest in three of the offers. The FBI was one of them.

After thorough deliberation, I candidly chose to work for the FBI because of its distinguished mission, benefits, and promotional potentials. Another reason is that it reminded me of one of my favorite TV shows from my youth, *Dragnet*, although there is nothing comparable to being employed by an actual law enforcement agency and perceiving the practicalities of the law and justice.

Considering the superiority and extent of work the FBI is obligated to achieve, it still exhibits profuse compassion for its employees and society.

While I have always had distinguished respect and generosity for people, the magnanimity exhibited by the FBI has allowed me to be more magnanimous.

During my tenure at the FBI, I worked under the management of numerous directors, assistant directors, deputy directors, supervisory special agents, special agents, and other executive personnel—I have reverence for them all!

However, undeniably, I declare one of the FBI directors to be an "emperor" of loyalty, bravery, and law, someone who will go above and beyond the call of duty to uphold the reigns of the US Constitution, rule of law, and equality. That person would be the former FBI Director Robert S. Mueller III.

It did not matter if Director Mueller was walking about the halls of the FBI or just entering a room; he has a notable bravura and an effective presence.

I recall, clear as day, during our annual employee conferences, he'd enter the room, greet the employees, remove his jacket and lay it on a chair, partially turn up his sleeves, then slightly relax his tie. Trust me, everyone knew it was time to get down to business!

Even though Director Mueller wanted the FBI workforce to be jubilant and contented, he made it clear, "When it's time to work, it's time to work!"

He reiterated, "I will not tolerate any deceitfulness, laziness, or discrimination. I require every single employee to honor their sworn oath and adhere to the FBI's mission. And if you did not join the FBI to uphold its integrity and tolerate the work, you're in the wrong business!"

Eradicating a reputable leader from a job without appropriate clarification is like confiscating all the coffee from a coffee shop just to sell the tea.
–RJW

In addition, Director Mueller is a first-rate crusader of loyalty, and we are privileged that he was appointed to explore interference in the 2016 US election, which also involved the outrageous firing of an existing FBI director in May 2017, a director who was aware of and unsettled with Russia's meddling in the US election and multiple instances of corruption regarding the United States.

To this day, I do not understand the rationality of firing Director James Comey while he was on official business at one of the FBI field offices.

The dishonor imposed upon him was done in a most awkward, uncalled-for, petty way, with no respect for the dedication, thoroughness, valor, and integrity he has exemplified throughout his civic profession. In all my years being employed with the FBI and beyond. I never imagined that an existing FBI director would be stripped of authority and covertly fired by a personal bodyguard.

It is unacceptable for a president, administration, or alliances to surpass jurisdictive or executive privileges to badger former and current executives, organizations, or institutions.

Besides, there is a code of conduct to follow whenever a public official is to be fired from an official role and duties, unless, of course, they are forced to be fired instantaneously for a severe misconduct or crime.

Nonetheless, we must hope that a decent individual who entrenches themselves in a notable sphere of the law and justice, who loathes depravity like Robert Mueller does, is within reach should the United States ever have its independent rights impaired by a foreign power or rival again in the future.

Justly, whenever the FBI headquarters relocates or renovates, I hope a consideration is made to incorporate Mr. Mueller's name into the name of the new headquarters. With confidence, I feel this will reinforce the FBI's dedication, bravery, and integrity on behalf of its future undertakings.

15
Forbidden Boundaries

**If you toss your sword to feast with an enemy,
the first meal should be served with a long-ended spoon.**
–RJW

The United States is recognized for extending a hand to other countries in times of need. Similar support is offered to the United States by its allies as well.

Unfortunately, adversaries do not care about the virtuousness of our country. Therefore, it is forbidden for any US official or citizen to negotiate backdoor alliances, receive favors, make promises, or generate expenditures to any persons, country, or US rival. Any compromise of this rule is *unlawful* and will be detrimental to the country.

Equally, exposure of US classified or sensitive material is undeniably illegal, unless it is declassified with prior approval from Congress or respective organizations or administrators.

Also, if a POTUS were to put the country at risk to court a rival entity perhaps, it would be one of the most dangerous, deceptive actions that someone who has sworn to protect the country could do.

Furthermore, the US high benches, representatives, and other officials (1) are obligated to declare felonious rulings on anyone who is privy to or liable for this conduct and (2) should depose every liable contributor from all executive standings and duties.

It is undignified to be deceptive;
it is more deceptive to be corrupt!
–RJW

Imagine this scenario. A POTUS holds an extravagant event at the White House and invites quite a few of the nation's rivals. A few US senators and journalists show up to this event but are told, "You're not invited," and then have the door shut in their faces.

Behaving toward US representatives, spokespersons, or naturalized citizens this way—especially, in the presence of a US rival—constitutes a degradation to the nation in the most calculating way.

The minute Congress accepts this type of behavior from a POTUS, be certain, the exchanges and actions that follow will be incontestably shocking!

Nevertheless, some will recognize this sort of action as the norm after being disregarded so many times.

16

Censure of Words

It is okay to have an opinion;
but how you express it makes all the difference.
–RJW

I have created connotations for the word *LIFE* by inventing an acronym out of it, each letter representing a different aspect of the problems arising out of the 2016 election. The undertone that I am using is a depiction of its lucidity. The parables are significant for the pessimisms that emerged during the current presidency.

LIFE

L = Leaks

When highly regarded, catastrophic information is disclosed by a reliable source, usually an insider, that source is obligated to reveal that information, even if they are criticized for this candor. This makes that source a whistleblower.

Laws were established to safeguard whistleblowers; however, these individuals must adhere to the guiding principles for those laws.

> *If you condemn somebody for telling the truth,*
> *you are compelling them to preserve a deception.*
> *–RJW*

A whistleblower cannot disclose top-secret or sensitive information to the public. There are protocols and guiding principles to adhere to, to ensure the evidence exposed will be secured and presented to the proper officials. If these principles are not followed, the whistleblowers may be putting themselves and others in danger.

I = Investigations

Selecting the ideal president or public representative can seem complex but encouraging and exhilarating too. It gives voters an opportunity to choose whom they feel will lead and advance the country in a liberal way.

However, it is perplexing to appreciate an election after the horde of investigations about the exploitations, disloyalties, and interferences that occurred throughout the 2016 presidency and election period, although, many of these inquiries could not be ignored and were extremely necessary.

Congress should enact a process for evaluating the temperament of every potential political representative. This process will discourage egotistical and illicit events from occurring during elections.

Technique Process
1. Acknowledge the problematic behavior.
2. Determine the basis of the behavior (i.e., person, place, or thing).
3. Classify the extent of the corrupt or illegal behavior to administer the penalties.
4. Advise guilty persons of the penalties they are facing.
5. Act to rectify the issue or enact the penalty within thirty days or less.

Three phases are employed to enact the penalty:
1. Phase I: the situation must be resolved within thirty days. If not, it will move to phase II.
2. Phase II: the matter is prolonged for thirty days to obtain additional facts and evidence.
3. Phase III: a call of action will be executed by the magistrates no later than forty-five to sixty days from the date and time phase II initiated.

It is defective to dedicate too much time assessing a corruption when, in fact, the caveats are greater than the exploitation.
–RJW

F = Fake

If someone makes a statement that seems incredible but what they have said can be confirmed as accurate, then it is not "fake."

If you pick an apple from a tree but the tree is fake and the apple is too,
it does not change the fact that a tree is still a tree and an apple is an apple.
–RJW

Advantageous information is valuable when it is provided by a dependable source. Even so, the source divulging the data must be able to authenticate its validity or it might be questioned or considered ambiguous.

That is why we must rely on those who are sworn to loyalty to ensure what's being conveyed to the public, country, and the world is factual and accurate.

E = Estranged

It was disturbing to see the division the United States experienced throughout the 2016 presidential campaigns, debates, and election.

As time went on, even a year past the election, the country seemed frozen, unchanged, and remote from being unified with no sign of persistence.

It is time that we stand up and bring the essence of unity back to *LIFE*.

17
Pathways to Reality

God buffers moral pathways against unjust mayhems.
–RJW

We should be enthusiastic and proud about exercising our civil rights to vote and elect the best representatives to govern our country and protect our democracy.

Nevertheless, we had no inkling that this 2016 election interlude was going to be of a substandard quality or how unresponsive we would be to what transpired afterward.

To validate our loyalty to the country and uphold our constitutional rights as devoted citizens, we must cultivate a mutual bonding.

[Action required] Write in the section beneath each word or in your "Reader's Notes" section of this book to convey your prime thought for these words.

This exercise is anticipated to highlight some of the events and tensions that hindered the current presidency. You can modify the letters if you need to.

To help relieve some of the political tension and up-turn the worth of this exchange, share your responses with your family and friends. Also, you can host a social event for this activity and entitle it "Apropos Realisms."

T = Treason

Notes: _____

_____

R = Racial Discrimination

Notes: _____

_____

I = Immorality

Notes: _____

_____

U = Unprecedented

Notes: _____

_____

M = Meddling

Notes: _____

_____

P = Partisan

Notes: _____

_____

H = House of Mayhem

Notes: _____

_____

PUTTING

(Stop! Read the bold words as a sentence from top to bottom. It may make you grasp at the assertion it conveys.)

P = Political

Notes: _____

_____

U = Underlying

Notes: _____

_____

T = Threat

Notes: _____

_____

T = To an

Notes: _____

_____

I = Independent

Notes: _____

_____

N = Nation

Notes: _____

_____

G = G Summit

Notes: _____

_____

[Action required] Close the book for a minute, then re-open it to assess the notes you jotted for *TRIUMPH* and *PUTTING*. Hopefully, you will be extra driven to partake in this expedition to restore, reunite, and revive America again!

18
Weapons Against the United States

The United States of America is such an outstanding nation and, I hope you can agree, a nation like no other. It is time to restore the legacy that makes it so celebrated.

Unfortunately, US rivals do not have the same esteem for the country as we do, as they constantly make attempts to demote our standing in the world. Even so, the goal is to remain sociable with US allies and hopeful in reaching solidarity with the adversaries.

It is important for conflicting countries to make treaties, but respectively, all countries must be willing to tolerate a mutual respect for the other country's scope to reach proper and equivalent goals.

When a US president attends global summits, it is propriety to make sure the appropriate witnesses are present to verify all discussions and that the details of the discussions, with limited restriction to the classified talks, are available upon request by sanctioned officials.

Besides, presidents must be copiously answerable for an inclusive state of affairs for their country and represent their country as a protégé with a noble purpose, specifically at high-level meetings.

During the 2016 election period, US intelligence agencies established that Russia hacked the US email accounts to interfere with the voting process. This is an irrefutable intrusion of the US traditions and a threat to our democracy!

If the United States suffers these exploitations without pursuing solid consequences, rivals will presuppose the country is susceptible to further corruption.

Therefore, the powers that be—that is, the POTUS, legislators, and other related officials—must improve and reinforce the techniques and safety procedures for imminent elections without any assistance from partial entities or adversaries.

Envision the hypothetical outcome of the scenario described below should the US Congress allow this situation to transpire.

Scenario

A rival country initiates a cyberattack on the United States in an election period. US intelligence agencies efficaciously confirm the attack, but the rival denies any involvement and blames the United States for being incompetent in estimating their election methods and structures. Then, somehow the POTUS opts to accept the adversary's disavowal of any involvement in these attacks and considers the adversary blameless.

Later, you receive a certified letter in the mail from the US presidential administration demanding you provide the following information to your governor by a specific time or you'll be penalized: birth name, birth date, social security number, and voting preference.

Afterward, you send this information to your governor who is compelled to provide this data to a subdivision of the White House to be downloaded into a massive database.

Wait! It gets worse…later you learn that the POTUS plans to let the US rival—the country that obstructed a prior election process to be exact—help the United States develop a new cybersecurity system.

Finally, remember the data that was submitted to that subdivision of the White House to be entered into that massive database? Well, White House officials must make that information accessible to the opposing entity so they can assist with the development of a new secured configuration of US systems.

***

The minutest materialization of this scenario would generate an infamous consequence upon the country that could effortlessly be emphasized as impulsive weapons against the United States.

I cannot even fathom the United States granting this, or any, confidential access to an opposing nation who had previously tarnished the civil independence of our country's voting rights.

Congress should firmly declare that the United States *will not* tolerate or enable activities that would introduce conflict or instability to compromise our country's election means —and had better hold everybody supporting such peril in contempt.

Divergences can be a cushion for repulsions.
–RJW

In addition, it is necessary for every US federal and state agency, branch of the government, branch of military, and the White House to be effectively staffed at the time a new president is confirmed.

Newly elected presidents are privileged to choose the staff they desire and designate each individual for a specific job, but the current official should remain in that position for at least thirty days during the transition to ensure that the position is at no time vacant. Any deficiency of a relevant position may exemplify a weakness in the country's safekeeping and proficiencies.

US overseers must stay prepared to counteract or stabilize any conflicts, terrorizations, and catastrophes in a proficient, fortified, and tactful way. Otherwise, ineffectual decisions could compromise the security of the country and reduce the possibilities of a favorable resolution.

19
Deliberate vs. Debilitate

A catastrophic attack on one is a disastrous bout for us all!
–RJW

Honestly, whenever I think I am closer to finishing this book, some political breaking news occurs, which seems repetitive in the current 2020 presidential election cycle.

I would like to address the devastations that transpired between the time the current president took office through the months leading up to the 2020 election period.

Let us say a prayer for all the victims, families, public service officials, and spectators who were hurt, murdered, or who otherwise perished in all the tragedies that have taken place throughout the aforesaid time.

Quite a few of these tragedies were caused by climate and weather-related conditions and epidemics beyond our control, while others were instigated by heartless individuals.

Folks who carry out hatred will dawdle in a "patched-up" ferry until they've been reformed to cruise on a "revitalized" yacht.
–RJW

In July 2017, the rally that was held in Charlottesville, Virginia, turned out of control and aggressive. Prejudiced protesters paraded in an uproar, clinching fiery torches and shouting bigoted chants. An innocent US citizen who attended this rally to encourage peace was murdered when a man deliberately drove his car into a crowd to create chaos among those protesting the bigots while others were being thoughtlessly attacked. Largely, this turned out to be a dreadful event!

This protest was motivated by sheer bitterness and hate. It was like being victimized by a hostile monarchy. The upsurge of this rally effortlessly ascended because of the inexcusable influences and behaviors that were discounted throughout the 2016 election period.

It is ironic how people desire to launch dated hostilities to provoke a surliness from bygone days in a makeshift way, despite the hardships and mayhem we have grieved and tolerated as a nation.

To evolve as a unified nation, there are injustices we must no longer tolerate. The only fight we should be having is the stand-up fight for the reintegration of our country.

Man has restricted authority; God has extensive and eternal power.
–RJW

Nevertheless, a president must be transparent, devoted, and grounded to censure acts of bigotry and reprove every entity that attempts to reinforce such undertakings.

Furthermore, laws should be enacted to reprimand activists who encourage chauvinism, rather than reprimand folks who flee to the United States for amity and survival.

Speaking of striving to survive, it was upsetting to see the misery, volatility, and agony that families, communities, and first responders endured during the dreadful storms, hurricanes, brush fires, and slayings that transpired prior to, throughout, and after this election period.

Let us say a prayer: "God, we ask that you bless those who have lost their loved ones, who perished in the fires and storms and by the hands of evildoers. And Father, please fortify their faith. Amen."

A community can be reconstructed; things can be replaced; but a life is immeasurable.
–RJW

While these climatic and merciless manifestations were very perplexing and incredible, God can still calm a storm in its midst and restore joviality amid society.

20
Voters' Principles

**Do not be snubbed by silence; let your voice
be heard by your vote.**

–RJW

After the 2016 election, there was a multitude of un-supported assumptions and claims about the legality of US voters and voting rights.

I'm not sure why anybody would suspect the United States of erroneous caginess of its voting activity when, in fact, it was made evident that it was Russia that imposed on the legitimacy of the country's elective proceedings, the core of our democracy.

Administrators must modify the voting tactics, devices, and procedures to reduce and eradicate interferences with the US voting methods.

It would be wise to cultivate a voting device that can only be activated by the uniqueness of an individual's fingerprint, handprint(s), a combination of the two, or chromosomes (DNA).

The prints or DNA could be imaged and stored in a protective databank that is controlled by a US institution, not coupled with the White House or any political entity.

I know this development is achievable since today's technical and operative capability enables society to regulate telephones, computers, vehicles, and other devices from prints or DNA.

I am truly convinced that the technical experts and geniuses of the world can produce a state-of-the-art system to empower electors to use their prints or DNA to cast a vote.

Folks who are eligible to send in their ballots by mail must plan to get their prints uploaded into this database in advance. But then, if a print was never imaged in this database and a person tries to vote, the voter will be advised and given enough time to resolve the issue so they can vote.

Once voters' ballots are generated and become official, the voters will receive confirmation that their votes were accepted, tallied, and computed.

Numerous prospects could stem from the enactment of this conversion, such as the generation of extra jobs and an increase of promotional opportunities for current employees.

Progressive Voter's Checklist
- ✓ Make sure you are registered to vote.
- ✓ Know your polling location.
- ✓ Conduct a preliminary query on your candidate.
- ✓ Know your candidate's greatest qualities.
- ✓ Ask yourself, "Why am I assured my preferred candidate will be a loyal president?"
- ✓ "What would I change about my ideal candidate, and why?"
- ✓ "What distinguishes my candidate from the other challengers and former presidents?"
- ✓ "If I were contending to be the POTUS, my catchphrase would be _____!"
- ✓ "Who are the top three I'd place on my wish list to be POTUS?"

Dr. Martin Luther King, Jr. would be my first choice as POTUS because he is a genuine portrayal of what a mighty leader ought to be.

Regardless of the prosecutions and tribulations that Dr. King faced, he remained steadfast and true to his dreams and hopes for the world.

Dr. King was a person of his word, practiced what he preached, and marched for the liberty, equality, and justice for *all* people.

While a cruel assassination was the cause of his demise,

his legacy will eternally be a framework of peace, love, and unity among all people. So, hatred will not be celebrated; we must remain mindful of how Dr. King innovated the dream of loving our neighbors as thyself.

Believe me, if Dr. King were given the opportunity to become a POTUS, he would have been enumerated in my "Presidential Heroes" chapter of this book. Still, he paved a pathway for all presidents to pursue: a pathway to lead the country in accord and to change the mind of folks who want to promote hatred and injustices.

Those who have a real sagacity and credence for the liberty, equality, and freedom for all people, and a profuse desire to lead the nation, is fit to be a Presidential Hero.

[*Action*] In the "Reader's Notes" section at the back of this book, create some character references that you would consider to be unique values that would distinguish your Presidential Hero.

"Reunifying America!" This would be an illuminating catchphrase for the next election!

21
Presidential Commands

**The president must adhere to the ideologies of
the US Constitutionor step down from
the reigns of the nation.**
–RJW

1. A president must not attack the integrity or dignity of a political contender, a former president, a judge, accredited generals or officers, congresspersons, government organizations, or private citizens.
2. A president must not suppress the truth about past or present misconducts.
3. A president must show dignity to all people, re-

gardless of their ethnicity, creed, political preference, or any other aspect of their individuality.

4. A president must be truthful.
5. A president must not revere another country over
   their own.
6. A president must obey a sworn oath.
7. A president must disclose individual income taxes
   prior to being nominated, amending tax laws, or
   imposing tariffs.
8. A president must assent to the proven evidence
   presented by the US government agencies.
9. A president must not engage in social media to
   insult, threaten, or sway any person or country.
10. A president must not partake in political or per-
    sonal vendettas that may perhaps compromise the
    country.
11. A president must not portray the persona of a co-
    median or a luminary in tragic or life-threatening
    events.
12. A president must be compelled to encourage and
    invigorate the country.
13. A president must not give honor to or compli-
    ment rival leaders or republics amid their crimes.
14. A president must not embellish or encourage a
    falsehood.
15. A president must not degrade or dishonor any US
    federal or state agencies.
16. A president must never betray the country for
    personal advantage.

17. A president must adhere to the equal opportunity rights for all persons and workforces.
18. A president must abide by the procedures and protocols that are established for employees who perform acceptably in their profession. If an employee's job performance turns out to be intolerable, then that employee must be advised properly.
19. A president must not use given authority to publicly embarrass or attack the president's own advisers or any sanctioned representatives to satisfy personal vendettas or to get revenge.
20. A president must adhere to the ethical standards specified for government officials.
21. A president must never conduct isolated relations or negotiations or receive consultations with or from a rival country without inclusion or consensus from the Congress and certified officials.
22. A president must not evade the truth to conceal misconducts performed by family members, acquaintances, or supporters.
23. A president must be authentic in the eyes of the people and the nation.
24. A president should not under any circumstance poke fun at, degrade, or criticize anyone with a disability or handicap.
25. A president must not perceive the country with sullied eyes.
26. A president must never defend hate crimes, illicit crimes, or be entangled in the plot of such crimes.

27. A president must not exert any presidential authorities before being formally sworn in as the commander in chief.
28. A president must not amend, reject, or disobey any fragment of the US Constitution and its principles.
29. A president *must not* deject, avert, or hinder an authorized US election or investigation.
30. A president must not display or instruct injustices toward any country, person, or culture for personal advantage.
31. A president must govern the nation without showing bias for any person, culture, or entity.

Every former, existing, and imminent president ought to review the entrails of this book to gauge their valued or anticipated suitability to lead the United States of America.

22
President's Serenity Poem

**A daily prayer is a breastplate to shield you each day
and give you something glorious to implore again tomorrow.**
–RJW

God as my witness, I must confess.
I must be far more solemn than the rest.
I have been designated to lead a nation
And ask God to give me the willpower to do my best.

As the sun rises and my day begins,
I realize that I have a nation to defend;
When the sun goes down and daylight ends,
I pray to God I have made amends.

It is time to sleep, but before rising again,
I know that God is in control,
So I must give him thanks again!
WAIT! That is not the end...
I only pray that I have done God's will,
So the voters let me vie again.
–RJW

23
Revelations of Sovereignty

If you praise God during the day and prance about the Devil's quarters at night,
subdued darkness may become your illicit light.
–RJW

Regardless of race, gender, or political preference, I'm sure you've heard of Satan, also recognizable by devil, Lucifer, or fallen angel—yes, the one who fell into the fiery pits of hell and ceaselessly pursues followers to share in his gloom.

Despair accomplishes its intent when it accumulates a crowd.
–RJW

Individuals have a right to be confident, but it does not give them a license to tyrannize those who refuse to boost their ego.

Still, when some self-confident folks do not get the attention they feel they merit, they become disappointed and feel snubbed by society, which can sometimes lead to exasperation and retribution.

Therefore, they seek out others who perceive society in the same way to initiate a revenge muster. Their desolate undertaking is to convince others that a right of theirs has been denied.

You cannot beget harm to your brother with no expectation of
meeting God's wrath.
–RJW

Brutality, servitude, and prejudice are outdated. Those who resurrect these atrocious acts can be well defined as evildoers who will *never* sway God's perseverance. They will *never* succeed!

This is God's world; we are his guests;
let us make use of our visit.
–RJW

Satan followers will never rise to the services of the Lord,
but if you repent to follow God, you can be redeemed!
–RJW

Folks who are maliciously violent, with no regard for another's life, tie in with the biosphere of fallen angels…in an abyss!

Needless blood sheds in torrents in eyes of vindictive souls
but doesn't close the eyes of God.
–RJW

24
A Bright Side

A foundation is like society.
It must be amassed, merged, and structured,
or it is fated to fall apart.
–RJW

The US Congress is the foundation of our republic. This body is intended to alleviate the disruptions that affect the democracy and citizens of this nation.

Congress is not a court or expected to lead as one since the federal and state justices are specialized to preside over courts of law. But when there is an impeachment, Congress is permitted to hold a magistrate's hearing.

Even so, Congress must not turn a blind eye to censorious or unlawful acts conducted by a president or administration.

Congress is obligated to preserve the declarations of the US Constitution, defend the rule of law, advocate for the equality of civil and human rights, and sustain and reinforce the foundation of our democracy.

Therefore, Congress is considered safe turf in the eyes of our republic. It is obligated to evaluate and resolve reproachful and unethical occurrences that affect the nation, like how hundreds of families are still having their children grabbed and taken from their custody at the Mexican border in pursuit of asylum.

There are a lot of occurrences that can be categorized as atrocious, but I, for myself, have seen the grief, desperateness, and despair from people who could not locate their children, extended family, or friends during a catastrophe.

There is strength in seeking the proper entities for assistance.
–RJW

Pardon me as I reminisce just a bit.

I prearranged a seminar for several FBI executives, agents, and administrative personnel. However, the seminar was canceled because of the 9/11 attacks.

Later, I telephoned the presenter to reschedule the seminar and adjust the agenda. I asked if the discussion could be revised to help the employees deal with the aftermath of the 9/11 attacks. The presenter agreed to my request given that it was in accord with the objectives of the original topics.

I renamed the session to reflect the changes. It was previously "Aftermath of Trauma" and renamed "Dealing with the Aftermath of Trauma."

The presenter came to FBI headquarters (FBIHQ) several months later to conduct the seminar. Amazingly, all the attendees, including myself, found the entire presentation to be phenomenal!

The attendees talked about the disasters they have grieved and their experiences and emotional state regarding the 9/11 attacks. One attendee told us that her brother was killed instantly when one of those planes hit the office building where he worked. She became emotional as she described the distress she still battled. Later, she said how talking about her emotional state and hearing about the misfortunes that others grieved strengthened her faith and gave her a new perspective on how to deal with devastation.

It should be remembered that every person who was injured or who perished in these attacks was somebody's mother, father, husband, wife, sister, brother, child, or friend. Of course, it is upsetting to lose a loved one, but when your loved one's life is shortened by a needless calamity, it is even more mortifying! So, to have your children taken from you, with no inkling of when you will get to see or hold them again, is irrefutably unbearable.

Now tell me, who should we look to for help when children are grabbed from you, shuffled around like thieves in the night, and confined with no hint of their whereabouts?

In circumstances like these, mainly if it is politically motivated, we seek out proper help from the representatives on Capitol Hill.

Besides, it is vital for the Democrats and Republicans to intermediate and stop these sorts of actions!

In addition, after the courts ordered the children to be reunited with their families in a specified time frame, it was absurd for the current presidential administration to stipulate that "Some of the children will not be reuniting with their families; they'll be going to foster homes to be adopted."

[Action required] Close your eyes and envision this. You travel to a distinct country, and your child, grandchild, or a young relative is snatched from you for so-called trespassing. Then you are told, "You had better leave this country immediately, but without the child, or you'll be arrested. However, your child will be detained indefinitely or will eventually be adopted by foster parents."

Wow! How does this make you feel? Just imagine how the parents and the families who have experienced this at the border must feel.

The United States has never governed in this way until now. US representatives are duty bound to behave as one republic to guard the Constitution by the instruments of our government.

Everyone does not agree on all things;
but everybody can come to an agreement on something.
–RJW

On the bright side, we have a better sense of how the government and our democracy works, or ought to work, and are more cognizant of the impact we have on determining who should lead our nation. Still, we must return to the basics of what paved the historic foundation of our republic as our present days will someday be historical. Therefore, it is essential to restore the condition of our democracy today for the sake of our future generations.

In this moment, we must reexamine the constitutional crises and dismays that manifested throughout the current administration to prevent them from emerging in our nation again!

Furthermore, be wise to know that no matter who the president is, or may someday be, whatever happens in this world may not always be upright but may be occasionally perilous or more than man can handle. As I stated in previous chapters of this book, what happens in the biosphere can affect us all, some more than others.

I am largely speaking of the unbelievable, dreadful COVID-19 pandemic, which was sparked by the coronavirus in late 2019 and had spread worldwide within the first few months of 2020.

Ironically, this virus germinated as I was finalizing this book. Therefore, I will not denote any extensive aspects of the trepidation this virus has caused people throughout the world.

Be that as it may, my heart weeps for the victims and families that suffered from this disastrous global tragedy.

Furthermore, every single person who stays on the front line of this pandemic merits a rectitude of divine praise. *Thank you!*

Ultimately, it was a blessing to see the doctors, medical experts, nurses, crisis responders, scientists, governors and senate, military personnel, educators, methodological professionals, and public servicers keep us protected, inspired, and functioning. *Thank You!*

By the time you reach this section of the book, I pray to God there will be a medicine instituted and cure found for this COVID-19 ogre.

No individuals should glorify themselves for a responsibility
they are obligated to take on;
folks recognize a job well done.
–RJW

Respectfully, not to politicize this tragedy, this is a good point to brush up your response to a question that I asked you in Chapter 5, "Constitutional Reliance." Does the president have the capability and valor to preserve and lead the country in a worldwide catastrophe?

Finally, whether you have come to terms with something congregating or noteworthy in this book, you can be certain that God rules the world and will prevail in every situation!

25
Unity Pledge

Let us rejoice and unite to gratify God, one another, and our country.

–RJW

Today forward, regardless of what I have alleged, thought, or done, I vow to honor this pledge. Also, I recognize that I am entitled to the universal array of God's bequest.

Also, I pledge to respect my brethren's rights, and I understand they have the same entitlements as I do.

Furthermore, I will not follow, defend, or support any individuals who inspire hate, prejudice, or violence, although I will assure them that it's effortless to get along and to recognize what we all have in common.

And, God, for individuals who refuse to accept this pledge, I ask you to give them the fortitude, means, desire, and compassion to do so.

God bless us all!

26
Reader's Notes

Acknowledgments

First, I thank God for being my Lord and Savior and giving me the strength and insight to dwell on a path of the inevitable to make some difference in the world.

Next, I would like to thank my parents for instilling in me how important it is to believe in myself and to always put my trust in God.

God, thank you for blessing me with my delightful parents, a caring family, and understanding friends.

Also, I would like to thank my special friend MMW for the cheerfulness and the one hundred long-stemmed roses. (Smile, my friend.)

Last, I want to extend my gratitude to my educators, ministers, managers, and those who have no idea how be-

ing acquainted with them has influenced my life and suc-
cesses.

God bless.

Sincerely,
RJW

Meet the Author

A teenage girl was awakened from her sleep around three o'clock in the morning by a glowing light moving about in her bedroom. She sat up and watched the light as it calmed the ambience of the room. Then, she got out of bed, grabbed a notebook and pen, and went to the living room. She took a pillow from the couch, sat restfully on the floor, and started jotting down notable thoughts about her grandfather.

At approximately six o'clock that morning, someone was knocking at the front door. She realized that she had fallen asleep on the living room floor with the notebook and pen beside her. She got up to answer the door. It was her oldest sister. Before her sister could say anything to her, she said, "I know, Grandpop passed away, didn't he?"

Her sister asked, "How did you know that?"

The young girl replied, "I just had a feeling." She did not mention the glowing shadow she had seen floating around in her bedroom earlier that morning or anything about what she had written in her notebook.

The day of her grandfather's funeral, the young girl asked the pastor if she could share words of encouragement about her grandfather. The pastor replied, "Sure, my child. Let me greet the congregation with an opening prayer, then I'll have you come up." She sighed with eagerness.

Once the pastor called upon her, her anxiety subsided, and she spoke with fervor and confidence. The onlookers were very attentive to what she was saying.

At the conclusion of the funeral, her mother expressed how proud she was of her for sharing such inspiring words about her "Grandpop" with her family and the churchgoers. She also stated, "God will bless you for that."

Moving forward. When this young girl finished high school, she attended an industrial college. While in college, she applied for quite a few federal and state jobs.

In the meantime, she worked in the fashion industry as a sales associate until her background check to acquire a security clearance with the federal government was finished.

Thereafter, she was hired by a federal law enforcement agency and worked for them for thirty years.

Throughout her occupation with this agency, she became an adviser, boss, coordinator, and comrade. She also discovered a passion for organizing fundraisers for colleagues, strangers, and anyone who may have endured a terrible, life-changing circumstance.

Her coworkers called her the office butterfly because she was regularly tasked to organize her section's office parties and organizational events.

Whenever these celebrations ended, she would ask, "Does anyone want any of the leftovers?" Then, she would distribute apportioned plates of the leftovers to the impoverished during her break. It delighted her to see the gleaming eyes and unspoken gratefulness of those to whom she presented a meal.

Correspondingly, every year at Christmastime, she would fix meal packages at her home to give to the impoverished on her way to work or during break time.

Knowing she was making a thoughtful difference to somebody's life made all the difference on how joyful her life and holidays were.

I presume you wonder, "What ever became of this young girl who had a divine notion about her grandfather's death and shared it with her relatives and acquaintances?"

Well, over the years, the young girl has become further polished, fervent, and faithful and has reserved her mystical insight by wearing integrity like a fine dress, bravery like a sheikh hat, and her virtues like a glove. All to the nines!

Devotedly, that girl is me, yours truly, your author, Rachel. That is right, I'm still passionate about my endeavors, motivated by the power of God, and enthusiastic to assist.

My convivial duty is to help everyone realize, "A child of God is able to unite the world in a virtuous way."